The Unbeatable

Spirit of Faith

GW01007128

GLORIA COPELAND

JESUS IS LORD

KENNETH
COPELAND
PUBLICATIONS

Unless otherwise noted, all scripture is from the *King James Version* of the Bible.

The Unbeatable Spirit of Faith

ISBN 1-57562-014-6   30-0537

10 09 08 07 06 05   16 15 14 13 12 11

© 1995 Eagle Mountain International Church Inc. aka
Kenneth Copeland Ministries

Kenneth Copeland Ministries
Fort Worth, TX 76192-0001

The Unbeatable
Spirit of Faith

No matter how difficult a situation you may be facing today, God can turn it around!

The doctors may have told you there's no hope. Your bank account may be empty and the creditors knocking on the door. There may be trouble in your family or on your job. Your problems may be stacked so high, you feel like you can never overcome them. But don't let the devil fool you. He has never devised a problem that faith in God can't fix.

Nothing intimidates God. It's just as easy for God to heal cancer as it is for Him to heal a headache. It's as easy for Him to buy you a new home as it is for Him to pay your rent.

Even in times like these when the whole world seems to be in trouble, God can bring you through in triumph. He can do for you what He did for the Israelites. Exodus 10 says that when darkness covered the nation of Egypt in which they lived—a darkness so thick the Egyptians couldn't see each other or move for three days—"all the children of Israel had light in their dwellings" (verse 23).

Think about that! If you'll dare to believe God's Word, you can have light in the middle of a dark world. You can have protection in the middle of a dangerous world. You can live healed in the middle of a sick world. You can live prosperously in the middle of an impoverished world. You can live free in the middle of a captive world.

But let me warn you, you can't do it by dragging around in an attitude of defeat. If you want to walk in that kind of constant victory, you must develop a spirit of faith and persevere in that spirit even when the devil is putting pressure on you.

People with the spirit of faith always receive the blessings of God. They may go through tests and trials but they come out supernaturally every time.

I like those odds, don't you? I like to beat the devil every time. And, glory to God, we can if we'll walk continually in the spirit of faith.

The Apostle Paul gives us some

powerful insight about how to cultivate that spirit in 2 Corinthians 4: "We having the same spirit of faith, according as it is written, I believed, and therefore have I spoken; we also believe, and therefore speak.... While we look not at the things which are seen, but at the things which are not seen: for the things which are seen are temporal; but the things which are not seen are eternal" (verses 13, 18).

Open the Window

The first and most fundamental fact these verses reveal about the spirit of faith is that it *believes*.

What does it believe? The Word of God. What's more, faith believes God's Word just because God said it—whether natural circumstances seem to agree or not.

That means if you want to maintain a spirit of faith in the area of healing, for example, you must start by getting your Bible and finding out what God has said about healing. Then you must choose to receive that Word as the truth. Don't shut your heart to it by saying, "Well, that's not the way my church teaches it," or "That's not what my grandmother taught me." Just say, "The Word says healing belongs to me and I believe it!"

Then keep putting the Word in your heart day after day until faith rises up within you and your body begins to line up with that Word.

"Well, Gloria, I tried that one time and it didn't work for me. I guess I just don't have as much faith as you do."

Certainly you do! The Bible says, "...God hath dealt to every man the measure of faith" (Romans 12:3). Since that scripture was written to born-again people, you can be sure that if you've made Jesus the Lord of your life, you have faith within you.

You may not be acting on it. You may not be speaking it. But it's in there and the more you hear the Word of God, the more it will develop and grow, because "faith cometh by hearing, and hearing by the word of God" (Romans 10:17).

Why is it so important to develop your faith? Because faith is what connects you to the blessings of God. It's the force that gives those blessings substance in your life (see Hebrews 11:1). And besides all that, it pleases God (Hebrews 11:6).

It's faith that reaches into the realm of the spirit, grasps the promises of God and brings forth a tangible, physical fulfillment of those promises. It brings spiritual blessings. It brings the car that you need, or the healing for your body. It brings action in this earth.

Romans 5:2 says we have access by faith into the grace of God. Therefore, if you want grace for the new birth, you must receive it by faith. If you want God's grace for healing, you must receive it by faith. If you want God's grace in your finances or any other area of your life, you must get it by faith.

I like to think of it this way: When you believe the Word of God, you open the window of your life to give God the opportunity to move there.

Oddly enough, that bothers some people. They can't understand why God needs *an opportunity*. After all, He is God. Can't He do anything He wants to?

Yes, He can. And He wants to respond to our faith.

You see, He is not like the devil. He doesn't force Himself on you. He waits for you to give Him an opening by believing His Word.

We Believe...
Therefore We Speak

That's what Abraham did. When God told him that he and Sarah were going to have a baby, Abraham just took God at His Word. In light of the circumstances, that was quite a step of faith. After all, Abraham was 100 years old and Sarah was 90 and barren.

Most people would have been overwhelmed by those problems. But not Abraham. He "believed God, and it was counted unto him for righteousness" (Romans 4:3). Even though in the natural realm it was impossible for what God said to come to pass, Abraham believed God anyway.

That's what the spirit of faith does. It stands in the midst of the most impossible circumstances and believes God anyway! Then it begins to speak.

It doesn't say just any old thing, either. It speaks the Word of God. When cancer attacks, faith doesn't say, "I'm dying of cancer." Faith says, "I'm healed by the stripes of Jesus. Therefore I'll live and not die, and declare the works of the Lord."

You might think, *Well, I'm just not comfortable with that confession business. I just like to believe God quietly.*

That may be what you like, but it's not what the Bible teaches. The Bible says, *we believe, therefore we speak* (see 2 Corinthians 4:13). If you want to change your circumstances, you must have faith in two places—in your heart and in your mouth.

That's why God changed Abram's name to Abraham. Abraham means *father of many nations.* So every time Abraham introduced himself after his name was changed, he was actually saying, "Hello. How are you? I'm the father of many nations." To most people that probably sounded ridiculous because at the time, Abraham was still a childless old man married to a barren old woman. I'm sure they thought Abraham was a little crazy.

But he wasn't. He was simply following the example of God Himself "who quickeneth the dead, and calleth those things which be not as though they were" (Romans 4:17). By speaking in faith,

Abraham was doing exactly what God did when He created the earth.

Read Genesis 1 and you'll see what I mean. There the Bible tells us that in the beginning "the earth was without form, and void; and darkness was upon the face of the deep" (verse 2). Yet God didn't look at that darkness and say, "Oh my, the earth sure is a dark place!" Had He done that, the earth would have *remained* a dark place.

No, God changed the natural circumstance by calling things that be not as though they were. He looked at the darkness and said, "Light be!" and light was. God spoke out by faith what He wanted to come to pass.

All the way through the first chapter of Genesis we see God creating by speaking His Word. Over and over again it says,

God said...God saw...and it was good.

That's how we operate too, when we're living by the spirit of faith. We say God's Word...we see the result...and it is good!

One thing you must understand. I'm not just talking about saying God's Word once or twice. I'm talking about consistently speaking words of faith. If you get on your knees in prayer and say, "I believe I receive my financial needs met, in Jesus' Name," then go to dinner with your friends and say, "I'm going bankrupt. I can't find a job. I'm about to lose my home. I don't know what I'm going to do," you won't get anywhere.

It's what you say *continually* that comes to pass in your life. So if you're believing God for finances, make it a habit to say things like this: "According to Deuteronomy 28, lack is a curse of the law. And Galatians 3:13 says Jesus has redeemed me from that curse. Therefore I'm redeemed from the curse of lack! My needs are met according to God's riches in glory by Christ Jesus!"

Then every time your bills come to mind, call them paid in the Name of Jesus. Call yourself prosperous. Call yourself debt free. Be like Abraham and by the spirit of faith call things that be not as though they were.

Keep Your Eyes on the Word

Right now you may be thinking, *I really want to do that. I want to walk and talk by faith. The problem is, every time I look at the mess I'm in, I get discouraged.*

Then stop looking at the mess! Instead,

15

focus your attention on the promise of God. Keep His Word in front of your eyes and in your ears until you can *see* it coming to pass with the eyes of your spirit.

That's what the spirit of faith does. It looks "not at the things which are seen, but at the things which are not seen: for the things which are seen are temporal; but the things which are not seen are eternal" (2 Corinthians 4:18).

Of course, I'm not saying you should ignore your problems or close your eyes to them as if they aren't real. They are real. But according to the Word they are temporal, which means subject to change. And you can be assured that if you keep looking at the Word, they *will* change!

Once again, we can look at Abraham's life and see proof of that. Romans 4:18-21 says that he:

Against hope believed in hope, that he might become the father of many nations, according to that which was spoken, So shall thy seed be. And being not weak in faith, he considered not his own body now dead, when he was about an hundred years old, neither yet the deadness of Sarah's womb: He staggered not at the promise of God through unbelief; but was strong in faith, giving glory to God; and being fully persuaded that, what he had promised, he was able also to perform.

Abraham did not consider his body. He didn't focus his attention on the fact that he was 100 years old. He wasn't looking at his wrinkled, old self saying,

"Come on, old man. You can do it!" No, he knew he couldn't bring forth a child. He'd known that for some time.

He wasn't looking at his own ability. He was looking at God. He kept his attention on the power and promise of God until he was fully persuaded that God could *and would* bring it to pass.

That's What I Call Victory!

If you want to develop the spirit of faith, that's what you'll do too. You won't consider the natural impossibilities of your situation—God certainly doesn't. Ken and I have found that out by experience!

More than 30 years ago, when Ken was praying, down in the riverbed in Tulsa, Okla., God began speaking to him about preaching to nations. God said back then that he would have a worldwide ministry.

It was clear God had not considered our bank account. We hardly had enough money to get across town—much less go to the nations! But God didn't expect *us* to fulfill that call. He intended to do it Himself with our faith. He intended to provide the power, the resources, the ability—everything! All He expected us to do was believe.

That's all He expects you to do too. *Only believe.*

Isn't that wonderfully simple?

If you'll just believe, if you'll just spend your time considering God's Word instead of focusing on your own limitations, you'll end up just like Abraham.

Exactly how did Abraham end up? Very well, I'd say.

He and Sarah not only had that baby

God promised, they also lived long enough to raise him. Then after Sarah died (at 127 years old) Abraham (who was 137) remarried and had six more children. He became exactly what he and God said he was—the father of many nations.

Now that's what I call victory!

That's what I call the *spirit of faith!*

Prayer for Salvation and Baptism in the Holy Spirit

Heavenly Father, I come to You in the Name of Jesus. Your Word says, "Whosoever shall call on the name of the Lord shall be saved" (Acts 2:21). I am calling on You. I pray and ask Jesus to come into my heart and be Lord over my life according to Romans 10:9-10: "If thou shalt confess with thy mouth the Lord Jesus, and shalt believe in thine heart that God hath raised him from the dead, thou shalt be saved. For with the heart man believeth unto righteousness; and with the mouth confession is made unto salvation." I do that now. I confess that Jesus is Lord, and I believe in my heart that God raised Him from the dead.

I am now reborn! I am a Christian—a child of Almighty God! I am saved! You also said in Your Word, "If ye then, being evil, know how to give good gifts unto your children: HOW MUCH MORE shall your heavenly Father give the Holy Spirit to them that ask him?" (Luke 11:13). I'm also asking You to fill me with the Holy Spirit. Holy Spirit, rise up within me as I praise God. I fully expect to speak with other tongues as You give me the utterance (Acts 2:4). In Jesus' Name. Amen!

Begin to praise God for filling you with the Holy Spirit. Speak those words and syllables you receive—not in your own language, but the language given to you by the Holy Spirit. You have to use your own voice. God will not force you to speak. Don't be concerned with how it sounds. It is a heavenly language!

Continue with the blessing God has given you and pray in the spirit every day.

You are a born-again, Spirit-filled believer. You'll never be the same!

Find a good church that boldly preaches God's Word and obeys it. Become a part of a church family who will love and care for you as you love and care for them.

We need to be connected to each other. It increases our strength in God. It's God's plan for us.

Make it a habit to watch the *Believer's Voice of Victory* television broadcast and become a doer of the Word, who is blessed in his doing (James 1:22-25).

About the Author

Gloria Copeland is a noted author and minister of the gospel whose teaching ministry is known throughout the world. Believers worldwide know her through Believers' Conventions, Victory Campaigns, magazine articles, teaching audios and videos, and the daily and Sunday *Believer's Voice of Victory* television broadcast, which she hosts with her husband, Kenneth Copeland. She is known for "Healing School," which she began teaching and hosting in 1979 at KCM meetings. Gloria delivers the Word of God and the keys to victorious Christian living to millions of people every year.

Gloria has written many books, including *God's Will for You, Walk With God, God's Will Is Prosperity, Hidden Treasures* and *To Know Him.* She has also co-authored several books with her husband, including *Family Promises, Healing Promises* and the best-selling daily devotionals, *From Faith to Faith* and *Pursuit of His Presence.*

She holds an honorary doctorate from Oral Roberts University. In 1994, Gloria was voted Christian Woman of the Year, an honor conferred on women whose example demonstrates outstanding Christian leadership. Gloria is also the co-founder and vice president of Kenneth Copeland Ministries in Fort Worth, Texas.

Learn more about Kenneth Copeland Ministries
by visiting our Web site at **www.kcm.org**

Materials to Help You Receive Your Healing
by Gloria Copeland

Books

* And Jesus Healed Them All
  God's Prescription for Divine Health
* Harvest of Health
  Words That Heal (gift book with CD enclosed)

Audio Resources

God Is a Good God
God Wants You Well
Healing School
Be Made Whole—Live Long, Live Healthy

Video Resources

Healing School: God Wants You Well
Know Him as Healer
Be Made Whole—Live Long, Live Healthy

DVD Resources

Be Made Whole—Live Long, Live Healthy

Books Available From
Kenneth Copeland Ministries

by Kenneth Copeland

*   A Ceremony of Marriage
    A Matter of Choice
    Covenant of Blood
    Faith and Patience—The Power Twins
*   Freedom From Fear
    Giving and Receiving
    Honor—Walking in Honesty, Truth and Integrity
    How to Conquer Strife
    How to Discipline Your Flesh
    How to Receive Communion
    In Love There Is No Fear
    Know Your Enemy
    Living at the End of Time—A Time of Supernatural Increase
    Love Never Fails
    Mercy—The Divine Rescue of the Human Race
*   Now Are We in Christ Jesus
    One Nation Under God (gift book with CD enclosed)
*   Our Covenant With God
    Partnership, Sharing the Vision—Sharing the Grace
*   Prayer—Your Foundation for Success
*   Prosperity: The Choice Is Yours
    Rumors of War
*   Sensitivity of Heart
*   Six Steps to Excellence in Ministry
*   Sorrow Not! Winning Over Grief and Sorrow
*   The Decision Is Yours
*   The Force of Faith
*   The Force of Righteousness
    The Image of God in You

*Available in Spanish

by Gloria Copeland

Pleasing the Father
Pressing In—It's Worth It All
Shine On!
The Grace That Makes Us Holy
The Power to Live a New Life
The Protection of Angels
There Is No High Like the Most High
The Secret Place of God's Protection (gift book with CD enclosed)
The Unbeatable Spirit of Faith
This Same Jesus
To Know Him
Walk With God
Well Worth the Wait
Words That Heal (gift book with CD enclosed)
Your Promise of Protection—The Power of the 91st Psalm

Books Co-Authored by Kenneth and Gloria Copeland

Family Promises
Healing Promises
Prosperity Promises
Protection Promises

* From Faith to Faith—A Daily Guide to Victory
From Faith to Faith—A Perpetual Calendar

One Word From God Can Change Your Life

One Word From God Series:
• One Word From God Can Change Your Destiny
• One Word From God Can Change Your Family
• One Word From God Can Change Your Finances
• One Word From God Can Change Your Formula for Success
• One Word From God Can Change Your Health

*Available in Spanish

- One Word From God Can Change Your Nation
- One Word From God Can Change Your Prayer Life
- One Word From God Can Change Your Relationships

Load Up—A Youth Devotional
Over the Edge—A Youth Devotional
Pursuit of His Presence—A Daily Devotional
Pursuit of His Presence—A Perpetual Calendar
Raising Children Without Fear

Other Books Published by KCP

Real People. Real Needs. Real Victories.
    A book of testimonies to encourage your faith
John G. Lake—His Life, His Sermons, His Boldness of Faith
The Holiest of All by Andrew Murray
The New Testament in Modern Speech by
    Richard Francis Weymouth
The Rabbi From Burbank by Rabbi Isidor Zwirn
    and Bob Owen
Unchained! by Mac Gober

Products Designed for Today's Children and Youth

And Jesus Healed Them All (confession book and CD gift package)
Baby Praise Board Book
Baby Praise Christmas Board Book
Noah's Ark Coloring Book
The Best of *Shout!* Adventure Comics
The *Shout!* Giant Flip Coloring Book
The *Shout!* Joke Book
The *Shout!* Super-Activity Book
Wichita Slim's Campfire Stories

*Commander Kellie and the Superkids*_{SM} **Books:**

The SWORD Adventure Book
*Commander Kellie and the Superkids*_{SM} Solve-It-Yourself Mysteries
*Commander Kellie and the Superkids*_{SM} Adventure Series:
  Middle Grade Novels by Christopher P.N. Maselli:

#1 The Mysterious Presence
#2 The Quest for the Second Half
#3 Escape From Jungle Island
#4 In Pursuit of the Enemy
#5 Caged Rivalry
#6 Mystery of the Missing Junk
#7 Out of Breath
#8 The Year Mashela Stole Christmas
#9 False Identity
#10 The Runaway Mission
#11 The Knight-Time Rescue of Commander Kellie

World Offices
Kenneth Copeland Ministries

For more information about KCM and a free
catalog, please write the office nearest you:

Kenneth Copeland Ministries
Fort Worth, TX 76192-0001

Kenneth Copeland
Locked Bag 2600
Mansfield Delivery Centre
QUEENSLAND 4122
AUSTRALIA

Kenneth Copeland
Post Office Box 15
BATH
BA1 3XN
U.K.

Kenneth Copeland
Private Bag X 909
FONTAINEBLEAU
2032
REPUBLIC OF
SOUTH AFRICA

Kenneth Copeland
PO Box 3111 STN LCD 1
Langley BC V3A 4R3
CANADA

Kenneth Copeland Ministries
Post Office Box 84
L'VIV 79000
UKRAINE

We're Here for You!

Believer's Voice of Victory **Television Broadcast**

Join Kenneth and Gloria Copeland and the *Believer's Voice of Victory* broadcasts Monday through Friday and on Sunday each week, and learn how faith in God's Word can take your life from ordinary to extraordinary. This teaching from God's Word is designed to get you where you want to be—*on top!*

You can catch the *Believer's Voice of Victory* broadcast on your local, cable or satellite channels.

Check your local listings for times and stations in your area.

Believer's Voice of Victory **Magazine**

Enjoy inspired teaching and encouragement from Kenneth and Gloria Copeland and guest ministers each month in the *Believer's Voice of Victory* magazine. Also included are real-life testimonies of God's miraculous power and divine intervention in the lives of people just like you!

It's more than just a magazine—it's a ministry.

To receive a FREE subscription to *Believer's Voice of Victory*, write to:

Kenneth Copeland Ministries
Fort Worth, TX 76192-0001
Or call:
(800) 600-7395
(7 a.m.-5 p.m. CT)
Or visit our Web site at:
www.kcm.org

If you are writing from outside the U.S., please contact the KCM office nearest you. Addresses for all Kenneth Copeland Ministries offices are listed on the previous pages.

The Unbeatable Spirit of Faith

You can walk in constant victory and beat the devil every time. How? By developing *The Unbeatable Spirit of Faith!*

In this encouraging book, Gloria Copeland shows you how to develop a spirit of faith that persevers and brings you out on the other side of every test or trial—supernaturally blessed!

So get ready for victory! Take God at His Word and you'll win every time with *The Unbeatable Spirit of Faith!*

KENNETH
COPELAND
PUBLICATIONS

ISBN 1-57562-014-1

9 781575 620145

30-0537